LAUGH-OUT-LOUD JOKES

TO TELL YOUR FRIENDS

MICHAEL DAHL

Raintree is an imprint of Capstone Global Library Limited, a company incorporated in England and Wales having its registered office at 264 Banbury Road, Oxford, OX2 7DY – Registered company number: 6695582

www.raintree.co.uk
myorders@raintree.co.uk

Edited by Mandy Robbins
Picture research by Eric Gohl
Production by Tori Abraham

ISBN 978 1 4747 5474 3
22 21 20 19 18
10 9 8 7 6 5 4 3 2 1

British Library Cataloguing in Publication Data
A full catalogue record for this book is available from the British Library.

Acknowledgments
The author and publisher are grateful to the following for permission to reproduce copyright material: NASA: 29; Shutterstock: 5 Second Studio, 9 (cat), Africa Studio, 11, BaLL LunLa, 23, barteverett, 19 (sign), Elnur, 20, Humannet, 8, Irina Rogova, 7 (toy), Kues, 21 (gorilla & skyline), Luis Louro, 13, 15, marekuliasz, 24, Milles Studio, 22, Misunseo, 17 (bandages), MO_SES Premium, 21 (plane), Oksana Kuzmina, 28, Nadezda Murmakova, 10 (otter), Netfalls Remy Musser, 19 (house), Ricardo Reitmeyer, 30, Pavel Bobrovskiy, 17 (red bandages), Sergey Nivens, 27, sianc, 17 (ghost), Sirikunkrittaphuk, 31, Tarzhanova, 9 (mittens), Vadim Sadovski, 10 (space), Victor Naumik, 25, Yellowj, 7 (lobster)

Every effort has been made to contact copyright holders of any material reproduced in this book. Any omissions will be rectified in subsequent printings if notice is given to the publisher.

Printed and bound in India.

CONTENTS

THE BEST WAY TO TELL A JOKE

What did the lion say after
he ate the comedian?
"I feel funny".

Your friends will all feel funny after
you've told them these great gags.
Improve your joke-telling skills by
dishing out the wisecracks. You just
might turn into a world-class comic!

TIPS TO BE A
STAND-UP COMIC

1. **Speak up!** No one will laugh if they can't hear you.

2. **Practise.** Rehearse the jokes a few times before sharing them with friends.

3. **Get your timing right.** Your audience will laugh even louder if you pause right before the punch line.

4. **Don't laugh** at your own jokes. Keep a straight face.

5. **Use gestures** and body language. Some jokes are funnier with a well-chosen movement.

6. **Watch other comics.** You can learn a lot from the experts.

JEST FOR FUN

1. Why don't elephants go to the beach?
Their trunks are always falling down.

2. How did the bumblebee get to school?
It took the buzz!

3. Why didn't the little lobster share his toys with the other lobsters?

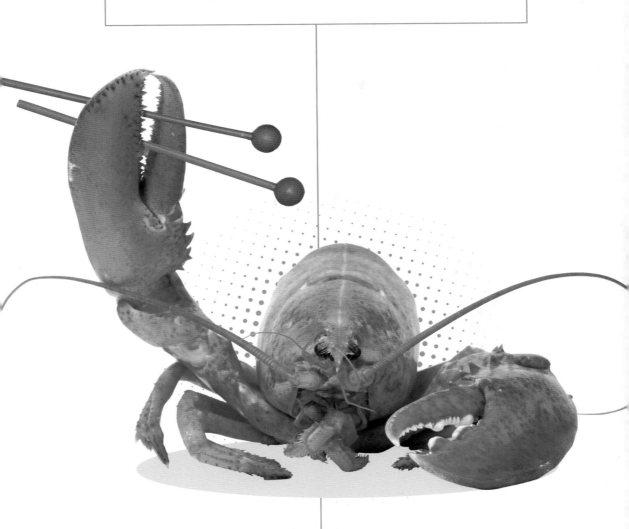

Because he was shellfish

1. Why did the basketball coach kick
Cinderella off the team?
**She was always running
away from the ball!**

2. What happened at the silkworm race?
It ended in a tie!

A TIE? NOOOO!

3. Why do ducks fly south for the winter?

It's too far to walk.

4. What happened to the cat that
ate a ball of wool?

She gave birth to a set of mittens!

1. Where do otters come from?

Otter space

2. Why did the cookie go to the doctor?

It felt crummy.

3. What do you call a train that

eats too much?

A chew-chew

NAME GAME

1. What do you call a girl who likes to play tennis?

Annette

2. What do you call a boy who floats on the water?

Bob

3. What do you call someone who
hangs on the wall?

Art

MONSTER JOKES

1. Why doesn't Dracula have many friends?
He has bat breath.

2. What did the Loch Ness Monster say to his old friends?
"Long time, no sea!"

3. Why is it safe to tell a
mummy your secrets?
**It keeps everything
under wraps!**

1. What's a ghost's favourite colour?

Boo!

2. What did the zombie eat
at the restaurant?

The waiters

3. What kind of fur do you get
from a werewolf?

As fur away as possible

4. What kind of mistakes do
ghosts make?

Boo-boos

1. What do you get when you cross a vampire with a snowman?

Frostbite

2. What do you say to a two-headed monster?

"Hello, hello!"

3. Where does the ghost family live?

On a dead end

1. Why didn't the skeleton go
to the school dance?
He had no body to go with!

2. How can you tell when
Dracula has a cold?
You can hear his coffin!

3. Why did King Kong climb the skyscraper? **He was trying to catch a plane.**

KNOCK IT OFF!

1. Knock, knock.

Who's there?

Santa

Santa who?

Santa letter telling you

I was coming today!

2. Knock, knock.

Who's there?

Radio

Radio who?

Radio not, here I come!

3. Knock, knock.

Who's there?

Isabel

Isabel who?

Isabel not working?

That's why I knocked.

1. Knock, knock.

Who's there?

Canoe

Canoe who?

Canoe come out and play?

2. Knock, knock.

Who's there?

Boo

Boo who?

Oh, stop crying!

3. Knock, knock.

Who's there?

Alex

Alex who?

Alex plain later, let me in!

4. Knock, knock.

Who's there?

Doris

Doris who?

Doris locked, and I can't find my key!

5. Knock, knock.

Who's there?

Noah

Noah who?

Noah a lot more knock-knock jokes!

OUT OF THIS WORLD!

1. How do aliens keep their
trousers up?
With an asteroid belt

2. Where did the space visitor
leave her ship?
At a parking meteor

3. How do you get an
astronaut's baby to sleep?

Rocket

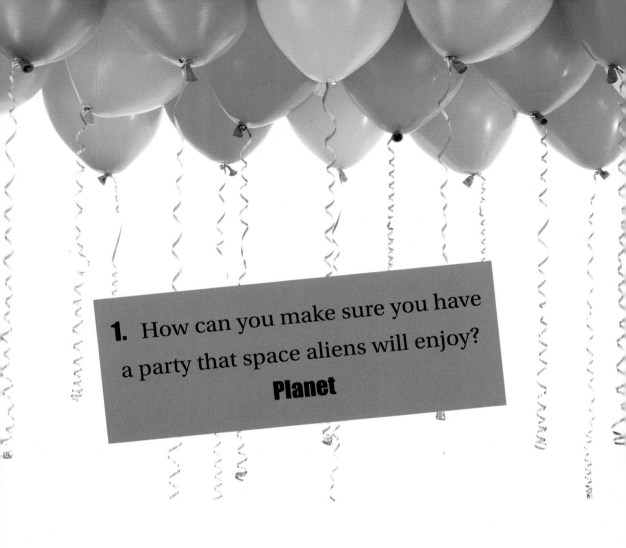

1. How can you make sure you have a party that space aliens will enjoy?

Planet

2. What picks up space rubbish where no one has gone before?

Star Truck

3. When do astronauts eat?

Launch time

1. Why couldn't the astronauts land on the moon?

It was full!

2. What is a light year?

It's the same as a normal year but with fewer calories!

3. How does the Man in the Moon cut his hair?

Eclipse it!

FIND OUT MORE

BOOKS

Laugh-out-loud Adventure Jokes for Kids (Laugh-Out-Loud Jokes for Kids), Rob Elliott (Harper Collins Childrens Books, 2019)

Roald Dahl Whizzpopping Joke Book, Roald Dahl (Puffin, 2016)

World's Best (and Worst) Knock-Knock Jokes (Laugh Your Socks Off!), Georgia Beth (Lerner Classroom, 2018)

WEBSITES

www.activityvillage.co.uk/animal-jokes
Activity Village

www.bbc.co.uk/cbbc/quizzes/bp-finish-the-joke-quiz
BBC

https://learnenglishkids.britishcouncil.org/en/jokes
British Council